Foreword

In September 2024, the Turner Prize returns to Tate Britain and London for the first time in six years, following successful and varied presentations in Margate, Coventry, Liverpool and Eastbourne. This year marks a particularly special moment for us: it is the Turner Prize's fortieth anniversary.

Established in 1984, the Turner Prize is named after JMW Turner (1775–1851), one of the most influential and innovative figures in British art history. It is awarded each year to a British artist for an outstanding exhibition or other presentation of their work. The prize has always aimed to promote public engagement in new developments in British art, and it has been a major contributing factor in the very considerable growth in interest in the contemporary visual arts we have seen in this country. Through the impact it has, the Turner Prize brings audiences of all kinds into direct contact with innovations in art that typically only people professionally involved in the art world would know about. The prize's forty-year history is arguably the most accurate barometer we have of new British art made over those decades. Its history encompasses several phases in British art history. In that time, the art scene in the UK has grown exponentially, as has its diversity and internationalism.

The members of the Turner Prize 2024 jury are Rosie Cooper, Director of Wysing Arts Centre; Ekow Eshun, writer, broadcaster and curator; Sam Thorne, Director General and CEO at Japan House London; and Lydia Yee, curator and art historian. We thank them for the insight and care they have brought to the research and selection process.

I would like to thank all at Tate who played a role in the making of the Turner Prize this year, in particular the exhibition's curators, Linsey Young, Curator, Contemporary British Art, and Amy Emmerson Martin, Assistant Curator, Contemporary British Art.

Finally, I would like to congratulate this year's nominated artists, Pio Abad, Claudette Johnson, Jasleen Kaur and Delaine Le Bas. We thank them for agreeing to participate in the Turner Prize and working with us on this exhibition. It is an honour for Tate Britain to be exhibiting such an inspirational shortlist of artists this autumn. Through very varied practices, all four artists reveal how the personal can resonate with the political, and how one's own lived experience interfaces with history and myth, nationally and internationally. In the Turner Prize's fortieth year, this shortlist proves that British artistic talent is as rich and vibrant as ever.

Alex Farquharson
Director of Tate Britain and Chair of the Turner Prize Jury

Biographies

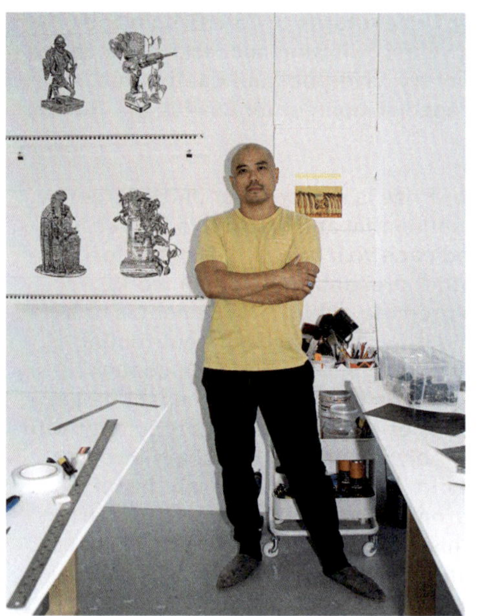

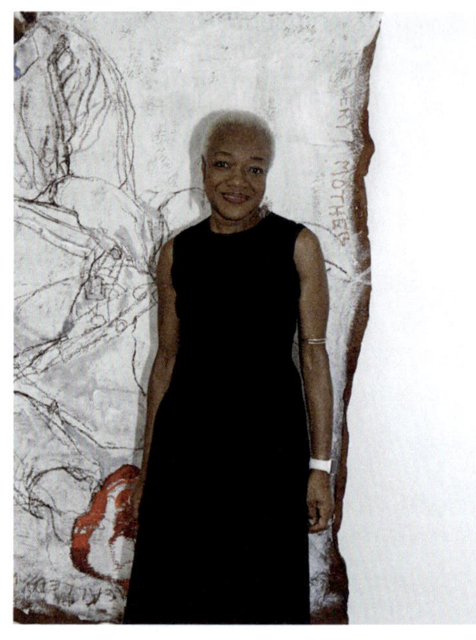

PIO ABAD

Nominated for his solo exhibition *To Those Sitting in Darkness* at the Ashmolean Museum, Oxford. Abad's work considers cultural loss and colonial histories, often reflecting on his upbringing in the Philippines. His exhibition includes drawings, etchings and sculptures which depict, juxtapose and transform artefacts from Oxford museums, highlighting their overlooked histories and drawing parallels with familiar household items. The jury commended the precision and elegance with which Abad combines research with new artistic work to ask questions of museums. They also remarked on both the sensitivity and clarity with which he brings history into the present.

CLAUDETTE JOHNSON

Nominated for her solo exhibition *Presence* at The Courtauld Gallery, London, and *Drawn Out* at Ortuzar Projects, New York. Johnson is noted for her figurative portraits of Black women and men in a combination of pastels, gouache, oil and watercolour. Countering the marginalisation of Black people in Western art history, Johnson shifts perspectives and invests her portraits of family and friends with a palpable sense of presence. In a year that the jury felt represented a milestone in her practice, they were struck by Johnson's sensitive and dramatic use of line, colour, space and scale to express empathy and intimacy with her subjects.

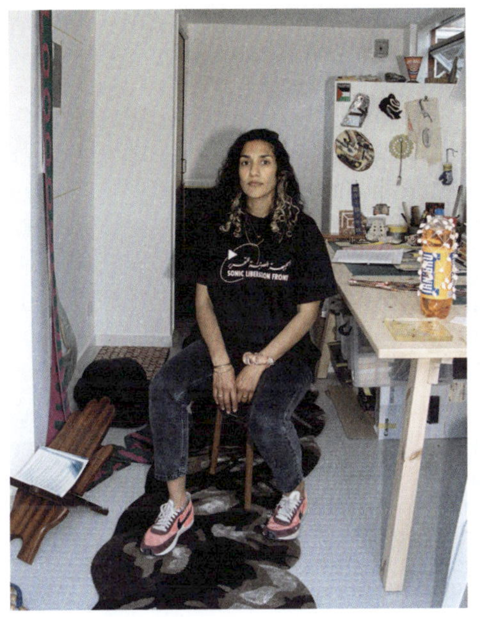

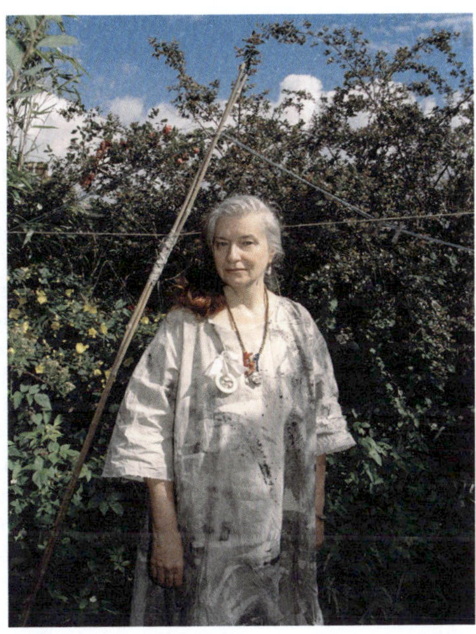

JASLEEN KAUR

Nominated for her solo exhibition *Alter Altar* at Tramway, Glasgow. Exploring inherited myths and political belonging, Kaur created sculptures from everyday objects, each animated through an immersive sound composition, giving them an uncanny illusion of life. Objects including family photos, a fake Axminster carpet, a vintage Ford Escort covered in a giant doily, Irn-Bru and kinetic bells were orchestrated to rethink the traditions and ideologies she grew up with. The jury praised the artist's evocative combination of sound and sculpture to address specifics of family memory and community struggle.

DELAINE LE BAS

Nominated for her presentation *Incipit Vita Nova. Here Begins The New Life/ A New Life Is Beginning* at Secession, Vienna. Le Bas transformed the gallery into an immersive performative environment hung with painted fabrics and filled with theatrical costumes and sculptures. Drawing on the rich cultural history of the Roma people and her interest in mythologies, the artist addressed themes of death, loss and renewal, inspired by the passing of her grandmother. Noting Le Bas's boldness at this moment in her practice, the jury was impressed by the energy and immediacy present in this exhibition, and its powerful expression of making art in a time of chaos.

Pio Abad

Pio Abad has described his practice as 'seducing people to knowledge'. Materialised through drawing, textile, sculpture, painting, text and the presentation of found objects, he creates objects and installations that surface repressed historical events, offering counter-narratives and alternatives to received colonial histories. Born and raised in Manila, Philippines, throughout his childhood Abad's family were high-profile activists against the dictatorship of Ferdinand Marcos and his wife Imelda Marcos and these early experiences of campaigning against conflict and corruption have shaped much of the artist's thinking. This direct experience of revolution felt within the home is present in all of his work, where complex national or global events are mediated through the lens of the domestic and the intimate.

The spectre of Imelda Marcos, a figure that the artist considers both a 'monster and a muse', and her impact on the Philippines while first lady (1965-86) is a recurring theme in his practice. Often remembered in the west only for her notorious love of glamour and excess, it is less often remarked that her lifestyle was funded by the theft of over ten billion dollars from the Filipino people, one of the largest thefts in history, enabled by the Western banking system of offshore accounts and shell companies. Following the February Revolution in 1986, the Marcos fled from Manila and were offered sanctuary by Ronald Reagan in a luxurious Hawaiian estate. On leaving for Hawaii the Marcos raided the Filipino treasury, absconding with an estimated twenty-one million dollars of jewellery which was seized at Hawaiian customs and returned to the Philippines where it remains, hidden from public view and inaccessible as a financial resource.

In collaboration with his wife, jewellery designer Frances Wadsworth Jones, and using scant picture documentation, Abad has painstakingly re-constructed elements of Marcos' jewellery collection in bronze and concrete. *Kiss the Hand You Cannot Bite* 2019 is an oversized concrete version of a 30 carat ruby, diamond and pearl bracelet from the collection. The sculpture is presented on a low plinth as though lying in state, a testament to the theft from the Filipino people under dictatorship but also to 'the many bodies that bear the excesses of empire'.

Begun in 2020, Abad's *1897.76.36.18.6 No 23* comprises meticulous drawings of household objects measured against British Museum collection objects stolen from Benin City, Nigeria

following a violent British occupation of the city in 1897.

A tropical houseplant or stack of cooking ingredients connected to histories of extraction is measured against a bronze figure or plaque 'tracing a narrative of dispossession according to personal and emotional dimensions'.[1] A similar tactic is used in the work *I am singing a song that can only be borne after losing a country* 2023, an intricate large-scale drawing of the reverse of Powhatan's Mantle, a decorated deer hide robe from the Ashmolean Museum. The robe is said to have been gifted by Wahunsenacawh, leader of the Powhatan Paramount Chiefdom to King James I to mark the first contact between the Indigenous American people and British colonialists in the seventeenth century. In drawing the reverse of the robe and allowing its lines and cracks to emerge as a landscape or map Abad creates an alternative space where one might imagine stolen lands have been reclaimed.

1. Ashmolean Now, p 63

Linsey Young

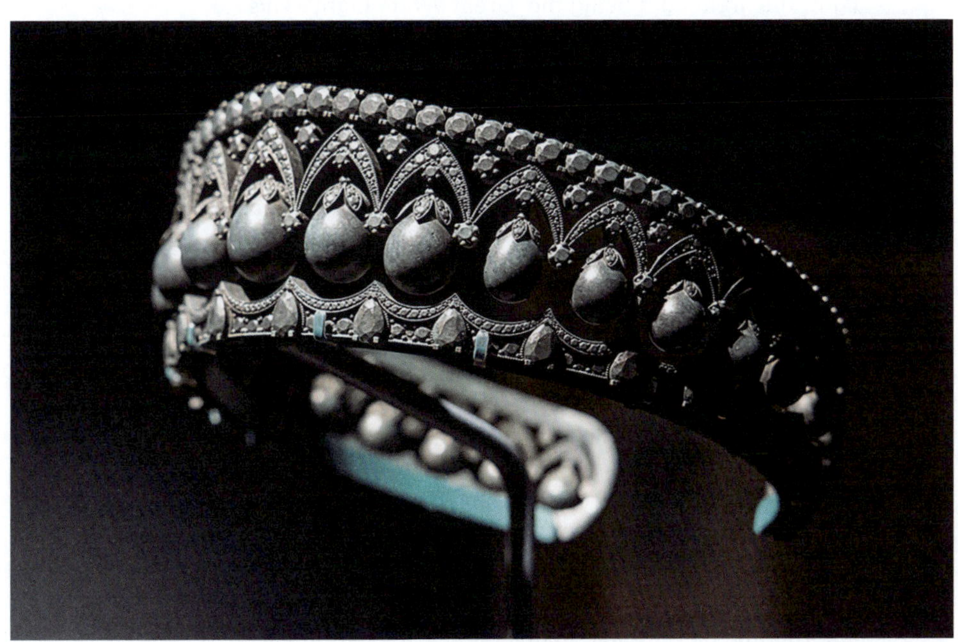

Pio Abad and Frances Wadsworth Jones, *For the Sphinx* (detail) 2024.
Courtesy of the artists. Hannah Pye/Ashmolean, University of Oxford

In Conversation

Linsey Young

So, my first question was that you were nominated for your exhibition at the Ashmolean, *To Those Sitting in Darkness*. Can you tell me a little bit about the title of the work?

Pio Abad

The title of the exhibition comes from an essay written by Mark Twain. Twain was a staunch anti-imperialist and he wrote this text called *To the Person Sitting in Darkness* (1901), which is a heavy excoriation of the United States' policy of manifest destiny, which culminated in the annexation of the Philippines as an American colony. Even the word 'annexation', which is the euphemism used in history books, is interesting because it sounds so benign. Like you're building a new basement or a swimming pool. The Filipino historian Ambeth Ocampo talks about having to call things by their proper names to be able to exorcise them. It's not annexation, it's the subjugation of an entire people. And so, Mark Twain parodies the American Empire's use of religion to justify this act of violence, of people sitting in darkness and seeing a great light, the great light being the 'Great White Light'. This essay is foundational in thinking about the history of the Philippines in relation to American history, and the larger history of empire.

In naming the exhibition at the Ashmolean, I wanted the title not only speak to people but also to the objects that have been witnesses to or residues of conquest. That remit is expanded in the title: *To Those Sitting in Darkness*. And it's also a reference to the fact that most of the artefacts that I showed at the Ashmolean in conversation with my work were things in the collection that have never been shown before, they have been literally sitting in darkness since they entered museum collections.

LY   What is your relationship to the Philippines?

PA   I was born and raised in Manila, and lived there until I moved to Glasgow when I was twenty-one. That's where my father and my siblings still live. When I was growing up in the Philippines in the 1980s, the country was going through a massive transition from twenty years of a kleptocratic dictatorship to democracy. My parents met as trade union organisers, working with farmers and fishermen in the 70s, and then they became very much involved in the anti-dictatorship struggle in the 80s. They spent some time in prison for their activism. When the Marcos dictatorship fell, they were then involved in this really difficult rebuilding of democratic institutions, which as we all know can be a very thankless process. Politics was always present at home. This was my foundation growing up.

One of my earliest memories, I think I must've been five, was visiting the basement of the presidential palace a few years after the Marcoses were ousted and exiled in Hawaii. The aftermath of their departure focused on the vast quantities of stuff they left behind, so much so that Imelda's shoes became a shorthand for corruption. These never figure in my work as I think they actually made light of the national trauma that was the dictatorship. Another failure to name things properly. The basement became this ad hoc museum. Everything they'd left behind was arranged on shelves and school kids would go on coach trips to see this stuff. These mahogany shelves are still etched in my memory. It looked like a post-apocalyptic department store. Looking back, I think this was formative in terms of understanding what museums are. They are...

LY   Places of theft?

PA   Places of theft and places of aftermaths and places where the arrangement and display of objects can shape how the public understands their world, both in a good way and a bad way.

LY   There's a deftness to how you handle the relationship between the studio and the home, the work and your life. How do you situate yourself between those two places?

PA   The way I see things, and I think this goes back to the family dinner table being a site of political discussions growing up, my work as an artist and role as a citizen, a son or a husband are seamless. My home is where work takes shape and my understanding of family and of history are entwined. My research in the back room of a museum or an archive sifting through things bleeds directly into my studio where I surround myself with historical objects of personal significance to me.

This also informs my approach to museums. I always try to find myself within these displays. I want to understand the vastness of how histories are narrated according to my own proportions. I think from that understanding of scale comes an understanding of my

work as an artist, working out why I choose to add more
things to the world. The studio then becomes the site where
I can identify gaps in knowledge, or gaps in telling. And then
the making comes in, the writing comes in, the staging of
encounters between artefacts comes in.

LY   What you were saying about proportions makes me think
of those drawings where you've taken the museum object
and you've taken something in your home and then there's
a measurement scale on the side and we're going to have
twenty of those in...?

PA   Twenty-four. These series of ink drawings are called
1897.76.36.18.6 and the title is a parody
of accession numbers in museums. Going back to this idea
of naming, the accession number is when an object is
baptised as it enters a collection.

LY   A very serious moment when you get your accession
number!

PA   The numbers relate to two things: 1897, which is the year
that the British Army invaded the Kingdom of Benin and
ransacked it, taking everything valuable from the city: these
were the famous Benin Bronzes, which were ritual objects,
personal mementos, even family portraits. The rest of the
numbers refer to the numerals in my home address. These
drawings came about after I realised that the building
where my flat is located played an important role in the
pillaging of the Kingdom of Benin.

LY   I love the works where they feel really precarious, where
you balance some books and then it's something and then
it's a plant and you're kind of trying to get to that height.

PA   The initial role of the books in these compositions was so
I can get to the right height of the Benin artefacts, but
then as the work was taking shape, they have also become
a bibliography for my life. As I was assembling these
stacks of objects, they have become even more autobiographical. The first drawing has the ivory mask of the
Queen Mother Idia on the left and on the right, a photo
of my mum that I normally have by my bedside is resting on
a ceramic couscous pot, which is then placed on top of
a book by Hisham Matar entitled *A Month in Siena*.
I have been working on the most recent drawings while
my wife and I prepare for the birth of our first child: an
early ultrasound and a milk bottle make an appearance,
on top of books on hypnobirthing and the C.I.A. involvement

                            PA

in Jakarta, among others. This approach has allowed me to be a bit looser because in the past, the practice has been so committed to forensically reconstructing objects. There's a tenderness in these new drawings that I don't think was ever present before. At least, not in the same autobiographical way.

LY   You're showing one work that wasn't in the Ashmolean show, *Kiss the Hand You Cannot Bite* 2019. Can you tell me a little about that?

PA   When the US granted the Marcoses exile in Honolulu, Imelda Marcos brought her jewels with her, stashed in her grandson's diaper bags. The headlines at the time were she arrived in Hawaii with diamonds and diapers. These jewels were confiscated by U.S. Customs and repatriated back to the Philippines, taken into custody by the Filipino revolutionary government of the time. As the governments and allegiances have shifted since '86, they were pretty much forgotten. Now that the Marcoses are back in power with Ferdinand Marcos, Jr. as president, it's likely that we will never know what's happened to them.

 Kiss the Hand You Cannot Bite reimagines Imelda's ruby, pearl and diamond bracelet as a concrete monument. The bracelet as monument becomes an apt metaphor for how this history has crystalised in my head, both as a larger political story of resisting erasure and a much more personal grappling with grief. It is both a body of evidence and an effigy, a body lying in state.

 I thought that it would be a really beautiful juxtaposition with *I am singing a song that can only be born after losing a country* 2023, the monumental red drawing of the underside of Powhatan's mantle, a ceremonial deer hide skin that Chief Powhatan gave the British settlers when they first landed in Virginia, reimagined as a map. This mantle that maps the many lands lost to conquest and the missing bracelet that monumentalises the bodies who carried the excesses of empire opens the exhibition at Tate Britain.

 I made this work with my wife Frances as I was still dealing with the loss of my mother, and this sculpture is very much a product of navigating this most profound loss. I am looking forward to revisiting this work in the show with our baby daughter in tow. She is named after her grandmother.

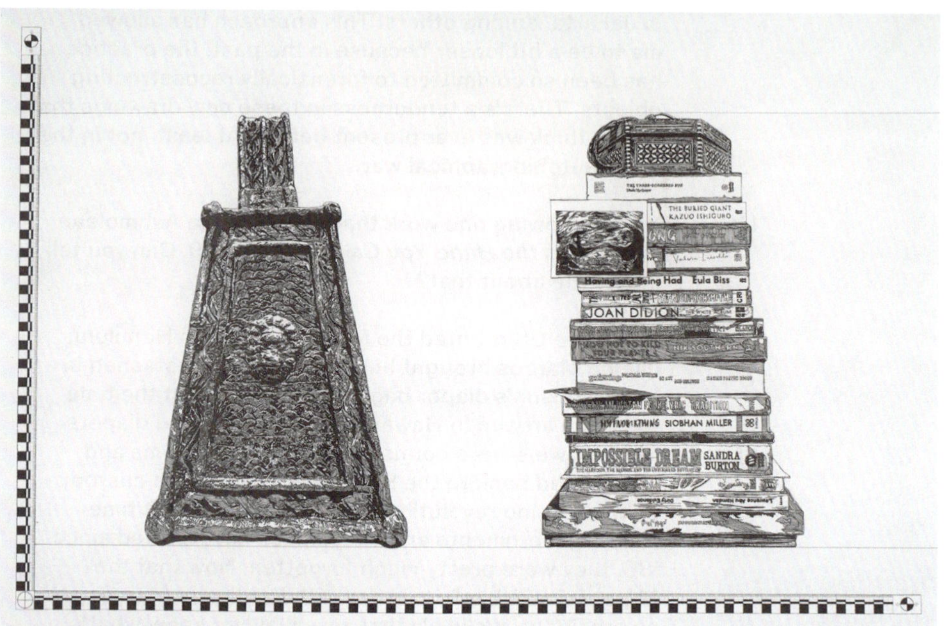

1897.76.36.18.6 No 23 2024, India ink on heritage woodfree paper, 1016×686.
Photo: Andy Keate

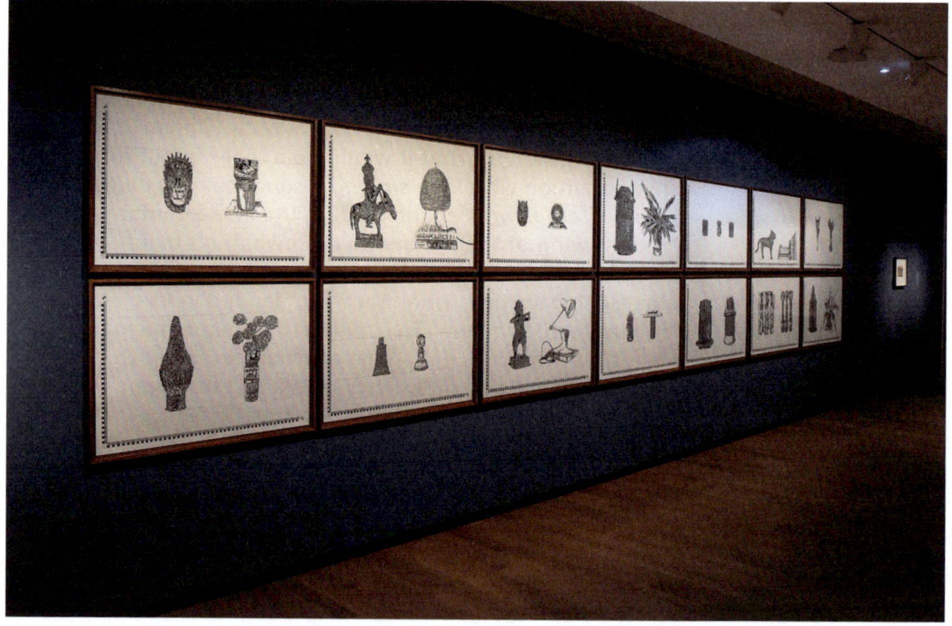

Installation view, *Pio Abad: To Those Sitting in Darkness*, 2024.
Courtesy the artist. Hannah Pye/Ashmolean, University of Oxford

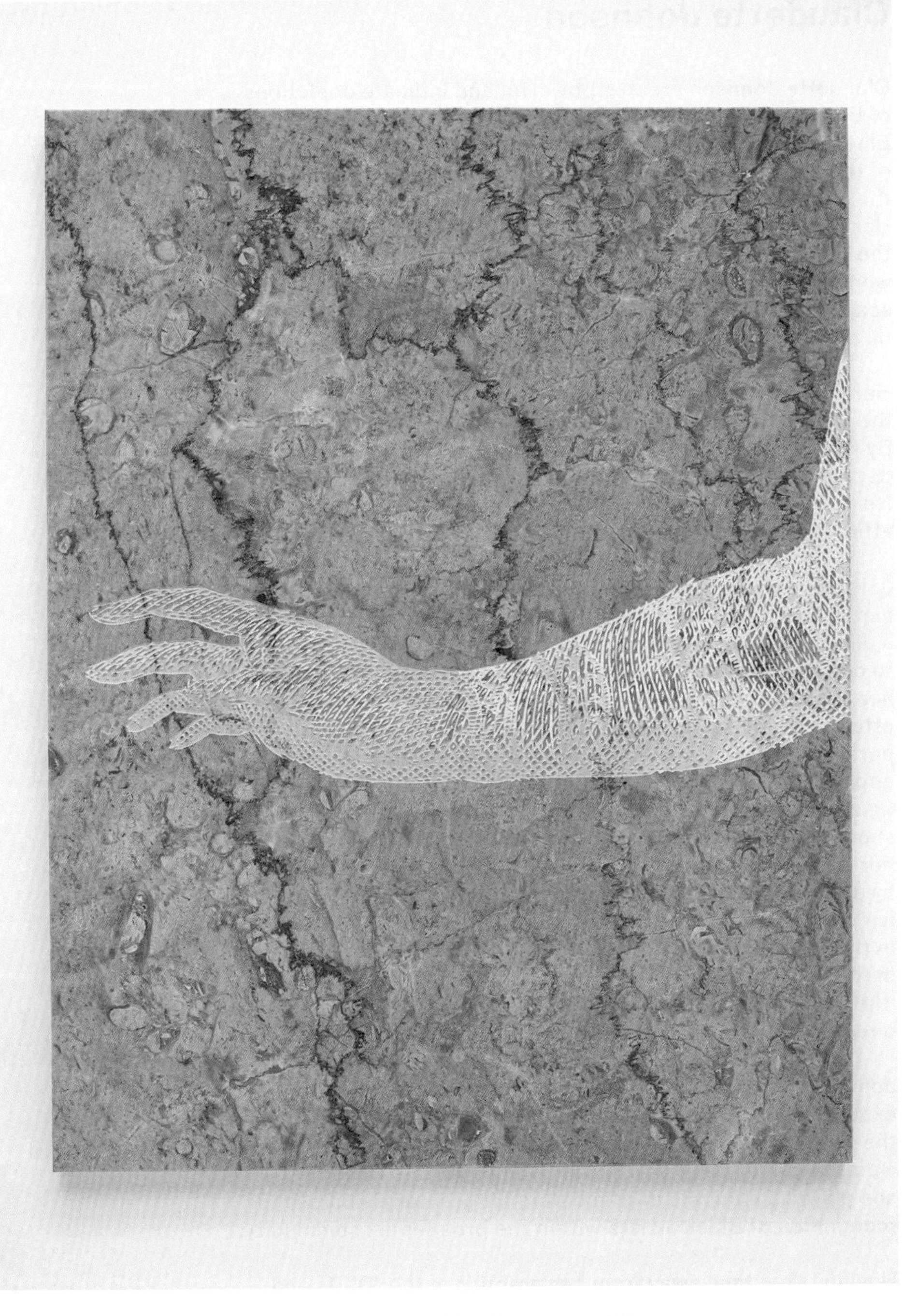

Giolo's Lament (detail) 2023, Eleven engravings on marble, Dimensions variable.
Photo: Andy Keate

Claudette Johnson

Claudette Johnson creates powerful and intimate depictions
of Black women and men that explore deep human connection.
Emerging as a key figure in the British Black Arts Movement
of the 1980s, Johnson has consistently challenged and expanded
the representation of Black individuals in contemporary art.
Her work is characterised by a profound commitment to celebrating
the Black experience. The figures are always present in her
works, with their unique ability to hold a viewer's gaze as they
scan across the surface of the paper. They appear to absorb and
fill the paper she works on, in a defiant and bold way.

Her work is not just a visual exploration but also a statement on
the social and political realities faced by Black women and men.
By foregrounding her subjects' presence, Johnson invites viewers
to engage with the nuances of Black identity and experience.
Her portraits transcend mere representation, serving as acts of
affirmation and celebration.

Johnson's works are well known for their, often, large scale,
meticulous detail, and vibrant use of colour. She often employs
a direct gaze and assertive postures, such as *contrapposto*,
to convey the inner strength and beauty of her figures. Through
her art, Johnson addresses themes of identity and empowerment,
offering a counter-narrative to historically marginalised
perspectives. The resistance to dominant narratives can also be
applied to the way in which Johnson refuses to situate her
figures in any form of space or time. *Protection* 2024, a self-study,
shows Johnson situated in a landscape which does not tie
her down. She noted that 'I made a point of taking off a watch
by a very well-known brand, just to make sure that there
isn't an obvious reference to the present moment.' The object
in the background of the work highlights Johnson's interest
in the medium and is an acknowledgement of her earlier works,
'the totemic form of Makonde sculptures was influential in
directing some of the more abstract work that I made in the 1980s.'

Johnson's contribution to contemporary art and discourse
extends beyond the paper she works on. She studied fine art at
the University of Wolverhampton, graduating in 1982 and became
a co-founder of the Black British Women Artists Collective, where
she played a vital role in advocating for greater visibility and
recognition of Black artists within the broader art community.

Having taken time away from her practice in the 1990s and
early 2000s, Johnson returned to making work in her studio
in 2014/2015. It was after this return that she began drawing

CJ

Black men. She has said that 'seeing an article in the newspaper about the death of young Black men in Los Angeles from a variety of causes including police brutality and gang violence' affected her deeply. 'I had my own children and I witnessed some of what they went through growing up as young men in Hackney. I felt very close to that story, to that experience, in a way that I hadn't been when I was younger. That led me to invite my sons to sit for me.'

This exhibition showcases a selection of Johnson's most compelling recent works, a number of which were shown at her exhibition *Presence* at The Courtauld Gallery, UK and *Drawn Out* at Ortuzar Projects in New York, both of which Johnson has been nominated for, as well as a new work completed this year. Together, these works highlight Johnson's unique artistic vision and enduring influence on the landscape of contemporary British art, giving viewers the opportunity to fully immerse themselves in the vibrancy and fluidity of movement within the portraits she creates.

Amy Emmerson Martin

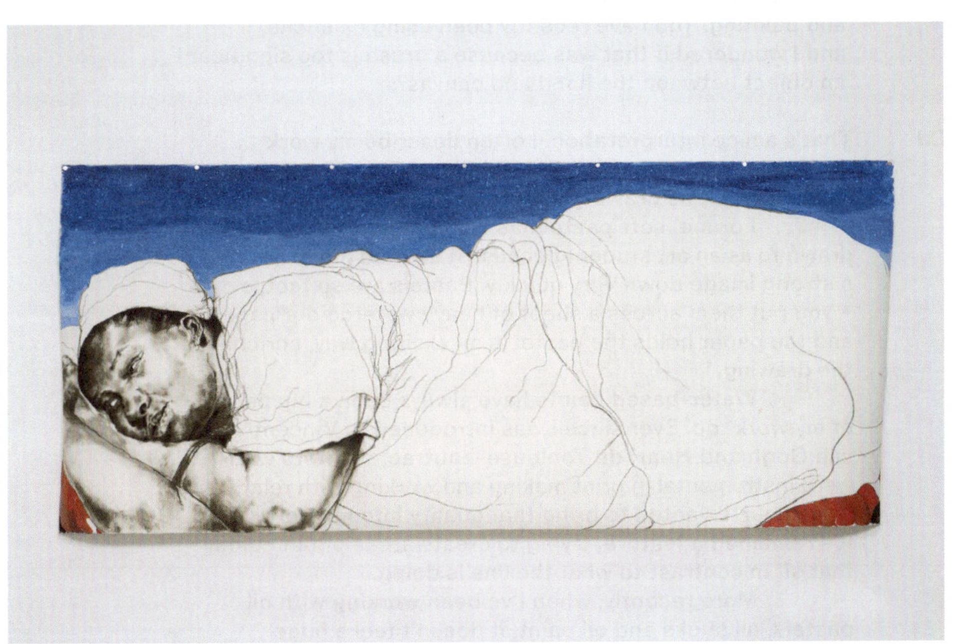

Reclining Figure 2017, Gouache and pastel on paper, 113 × 257 cm
Photo: Andy Keate, Private collection, London

In Conversation

Amy Emmerson Martin

I feel that your work sits outside of traditional portraiture, but it's what people naturally lean towards as a term. What would you call it?

Claudette Johnson

There's something settled about the tradition of portraiture that goes against what I'm trying to do. In traditional portraiture, the figure sits in an environment that gives you information about the character or social status of the subject. I suppose I've lifted my figures out of their environment and displaced them. That's a signal to my interest in the diasporic experience and the fact that we have been displaced and repositioned in a different environment.

Once I decided that my figures would be displaced, I found it exciting formally to think about the boundaries that the figure sits within, and how the figure might escape them. It became less about trying to tell the story of a particular personality and more that each figure was part of a larger story, almost symbolic of something bigger.

AEM The work is at another crossroads too, between drawing and painting. You have recently been using oil sticks, and I wondered if that was because a brush is too significant an object between the hand and canvas?

CJ That's a nice interpretation. I often describe my work as drawings, but they are also paintings. There is often as much paint as drawing material on the sheet.

For me, soft pastel has an immediacy that I was drawn to as an art student because it allowed me to get a strong image down very quickly. Pastels are so tactile – you put them across a sheet of heavy watercolour paper and the paper holds the pastel in an exciting way, enriching the drawing.

Water-based paints have always been a big part of my work too. Ever since I was introduced to Vincent van Gogh and Henri de Toulouse-Lautrec, painters who were instrumental in print making and working with relatively flat colour, I wanted to bring that quality into my work. It's remained a feature, trying to create areas of flat colour that sit in contrast to what the line is doing.

More recently, when I've been working with oil pastels, oil sticks and oil paint, it doesn't feel a huge leap from drawing. I call my work drawings or paintings interchangeably without any real commitment to one or the other. But because I began with drawing back in the 1980s, I suppose that's the first description I'd give them.

AEM   You've spoken in the past about your love of sculpture. Looking at the materials you use and the marks you make, it feels sculptural on the paper.

CJ   I've heard the drawings described as having a sculptural quality to them before. It's not something I consciously aim for, but the way that I work the pastels into the paper, it feels as if I'm moulding the figure out of the pastels rather than simply laying or drawing a line.

I'm not well-versed enough in sculpture to say how influential it has been for me. I love Barbara Hepworth, and Michelangelo's *David* still moves me. One of the tutors I found most helpful on my degree course was a sculptor. He introduced me to wood carving, and I made a few relief carvings when I was a second-year student. I remember looking at South African sculpture, particularly an artist working in London called Pitika Ntuli whose work excited me, as well as Makonde sculpture from eastern Africa. I think the intricately interlocking figures and totemic form of Makonde sculpture were influential in directing some of the more abstract work that I made in the 1980s.

Because I am a painter, the three-dimensionality of the work has to be convincing. I suppose that illusionist aspect is important to me and, at the same time, it's not the main driver. When I try to put my finger on the main driver, I find it hard to locate. It's somewhere between a fluid approach to drawing and the strength and weight of sculpture that give the figures a sense of boldly being here. But they're not fixed, there's a moment that is changing and evolving around them.

AEM   I sense a tension in your portraits, even in the way the figures are placed: they're twisted, in *contrapposto*, they sometimes feel confrontational, even. Why create this tension?

CJ   I sometimes want to confound the viewer's expectation of what a drawing of a person might offer. I have it in my head that portraits tend to be a frozen moment in time, that there's something still, predictable and sure about portraits in that tradition. I wanted to put the figure in a position that was, to some extent, destabilising. I suppose I want to have my cake and eat it, because I also want the subject to be solidly present.

AEM   So, it's about slippage?

CJ   That's right. I want there to be an inescapability to this
        encounter with a figure. Because there is nothing else
        in play except the figure, that forces a certain type of
        confrontation. I ask my sitters sometimes to twist towards
        or away from me, and then look back towards me, and
        this creates a spiral that's right within the sense of the
        work. I think this aspect reveals itself when people sit
        with the work.

AEM   Painting and drawing women has been a consistent focus
        for you, but more recently you've introduced male
        subjects. Why did you start drawing men?

CJ   It's difficult to identify the moment when I decided I would
        have images of men in my work. Perhaps one transitional
        moment was seeing an article in the newspaper about the
        death of young Black men in Los Angeles from causes
        including police brutality and gang violence. I was very
        affected by that story, as well as a particularly violent
        image of a young man who had been shot seven times, but
        survived. In the photograph, he's lifted his shirt to show
        the bullet wounds, and the expression on his face was a
        mixture of pride, and a sense of having escaped death.
        I guess I became aware of mortality.
                When I started out as an artist in the 1980s,
        I was involved with women's groups and Black women's
        movements, such as OWAAD (Organisation of Women
        of African and Asian Descent). I felt like Black women
        needed to be visible and I felt, for want of a better phrase,
        that we were at the bottom of the pile. So, I wanted my
        work to be peopled with Black women.
                By the late 2000s, that was changing because I
        had my own children and I witnessed some of what they
        went through growing up as young men in Hackney. I felt
        very close to that story, to that experience, in a way that
        I hadn't been when I was younger. That led me to invite
        my sons to sit for me. When I came back into making work,
        around 2014/2015, I needed sitters, and I mostly like
        working with people that I know at least a little bit. I had
        my sons sit for me because it's a comfortable relationship
        and it was an easy way of drawing men for the first time.

AEM   You mentioned earlier that you took some time away from
        art, and then you returned in 2014/2015. Why did you take
        time away, and how did you feel returning to the studio?

CJ   As happens for many people, initially I wasn't consciously

                              CJ

trying to take time away, it was more that my day-to-day responsibilities as a mother, and as someone who needs to earn a living, took precedence. It became more and more difficult to juggle studio time with doing various jobs and my children. So gradually, art got moved to the backburner.

AEM   I think all mothers put things on hold...

CJ   One image that has stayed with me is that I'd have a drawing pad out, and I'd be putting the children to bed, and I would think: 'When I've put them to bed, I'll come back and I'll do the drawing'. And then, invariably, I'd read them a story, fall asleep with them, and then that moment would have gone.

When I look back, I also think part of it was a waning confidence in my work. I was being invited to take part in fewer and fewer shows, and eventually none at all. I felt pretty much forgotten. I had work sitting in the hallway, under the bed, in someone else's cellar, and it felt as if it wasn't wanted.

It was only through the intervention of the artist Lubaina Himid that things changed. In 2015, she invited me to take part in the exhibition *Carte de Visite* at Hollybush Gardens. That experience reminded me that I could still make images that more than one person was interested in seeing. It was so exciting to realise that this little creative light, which had faded over those years, hadn't been extinguished. I was still taking things in during that time, thinking creatively, which made it possible to return with those interests intact.

When I was in my twenties, I had a kind of arrogance about my work; I was pretty sure of myself in that specific area. Now, although I have a different kind of assurance, I ask myself a lot more questions about the work than I did back then, and I invite questions from other people too. I like having people look at the work at a certain stage and getting their feedback. I could never have done as a twenty-year-old.

AEM   What are you currently enjoying outside of visual art?

CJ   I'm always reading at least three books. Currently, it's *The List* (2023) by Yomi Adegoke, a shortish story by Dostoevsky and I'm halfway through *Fledgling* (2005) by Octavia E. Butler. I listen to reggae in the studio, especially if I'm feeling energised about the work. But I also listen to R&B, jazz, classical at times, folk. My taste is particularly eclectic. It all depends on the moment.

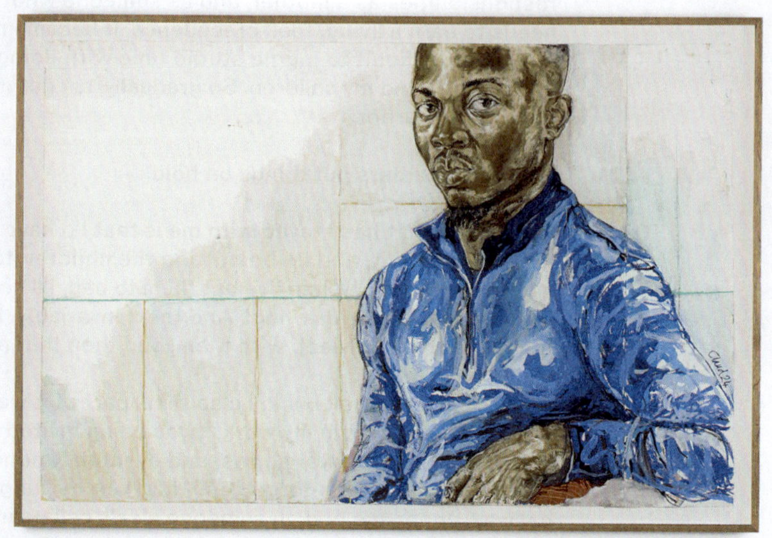

Young Man in Blue 2024, Pastels, gouache, pencil, watercolour with gesso ground on paper, 122×183 cm, Photo: Andy Keate, Hollybush Gardens, London

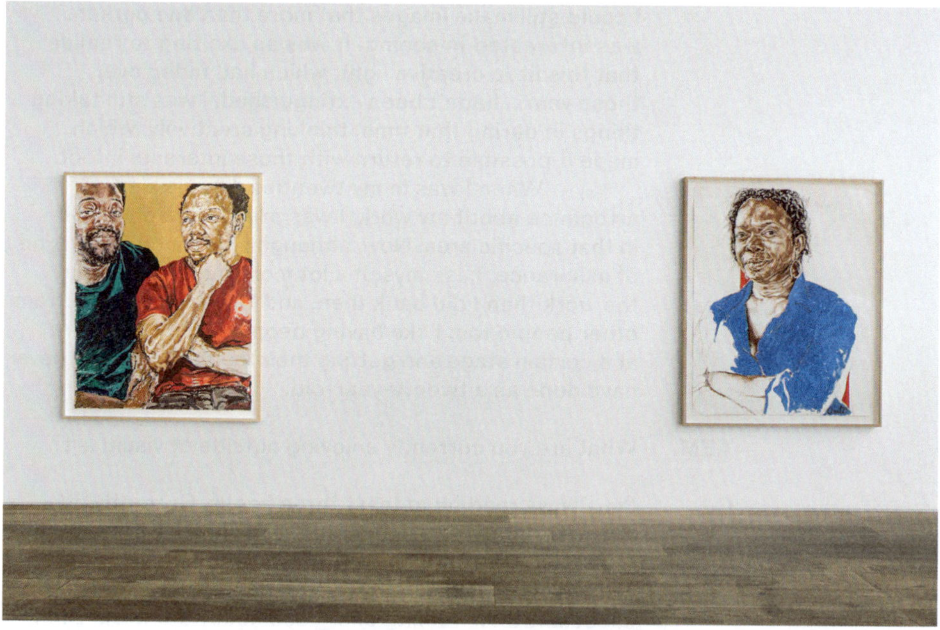

Installation view of Claudette Johnson, *Presence*, at The Courtauld Gallery, 2023. Courtesy the artist and Hollybush Gardens, London. © The Courtauld. Photo: David Bebber

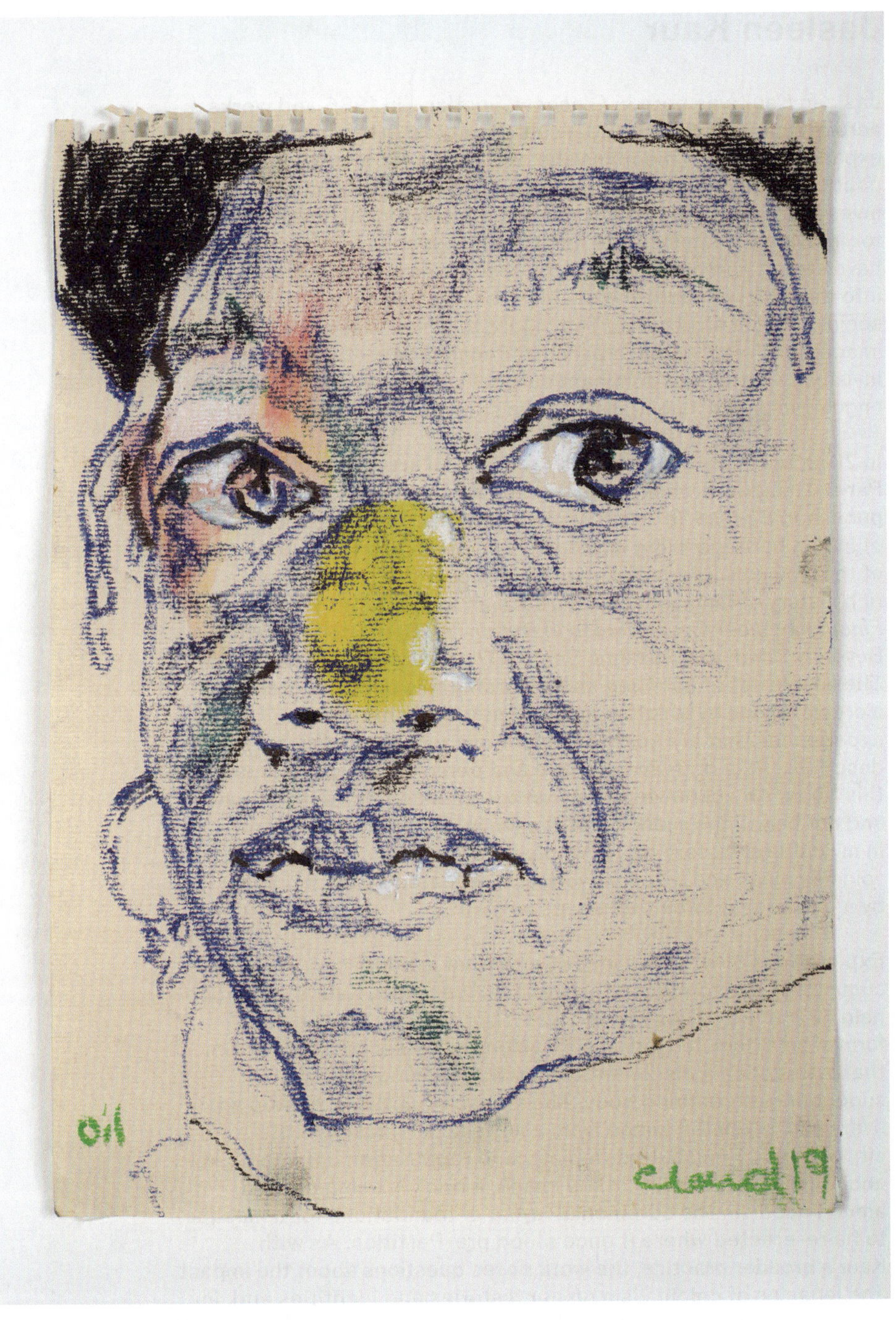

Oil Sketch 2019, Oil pastel on paper, 29.7 × 21 cm
Photo: Andy Keate, Hollybush Gardens, London

Jasleen Kaur

Jasleen Kaur was born in Glasgow, Scotland in 1986 and works across sculpture, installation, sound and text. Through this expansive range of mediums she explores cultural memory and political belonging, often working with everyday objects to investigate symbols and images and the allegorical power they hold for individuals, families and communities. Many of her assemblages have strong personal and cultural resonance and by bringing them into the gallery space, she enables them to interact with broader socio-political structures. The extent to which these objects or images are 'read' within a particular community – their visibility or invisibility within our dominant cultural landscape – relates to the ongoing impact of imperialism on the stories and histories we inherit.

In 2019, in collaboration with the curatorial arts organisation Panel, Glasgow Women's Library and Dent-de-Leone, Kaur published *Be Like Teflon*, a book of conversations between women of Indian heritage living in the UK. The published texts, born out of the women's informal conversations over food, connect to a rich history of feminist activism, such as that of Amrit Wilson's text *Finding a Voice: Asian Women in Britain* (1978) or Stella Dadzie, Beverley Bryan and Suzanne Scafe's *The Heart of the Race* (1985). The simple act of listening and recording this dialogue creates a crucial space in which to acknowledge and share women's lived experiences that are so often lost or overlooked. As the artist describes, 'It is both an inherited and personal trauma that drives this book. An acknowledgment of the silences, what is not said and not heard, the silencing of women in my life and, as I learn, in my cultural history too. A whole heritage of mistreatment, voicelessness and disempowerment, repeated again and again by a patriarchal force that keeps us quiet.'

Explorations of what is silenced and what is nourished by a community are continued throughout *Alter Altar*, Kaur's exhibition held at Tramway, Glasgow in 2023. *(Untitled)* 2023 takes the form of an automated Indian harmonium, a popular colonial instrument that introduces a dissonant drone, with moving bellows suggesting a breathing body. The kinetic sculpture sits atop an oversized, pixelated image from a news article, taken in the city of Moga, Panjab, that depicts land repatriation between Sikh and Muslim neighbours. In the image, a brick is being passed among hands in the ceremonial laying of foundations for a mosque to be re-erected where it once stood pre-Partition. As with Kaur's broader practice, the work poses questions about the impact and legacies of colonialism on our histories and identities and, in particular, on what survives and what is held close amid the violence of Imperialism.

JK

The harmonium in *(Untitled)* is programmed to play in dialogue with other sound works, including *Yearnings* 2023, which features improvised vocals by the artist that were developed as part of her long-standing singing practice. Working closely with vocal teacher Marged Siôn, Kaur used the work to explore embodied voice techniques and devotional singing traditions. We hear a chorus repeating 'looooooonging', and 'I am chooooorus' resounds like a chant or spell. The immersive work is installed in relation to a large-scale suspended ceiling, *Begampura* 2023. The name Begampura relates to the fourteenth-century poet Guru Ravidas' utopian vision of a casteless, classless and stateless society or 'a place with no pain'. The structure is printed with an image of the sky from Pollok Park in Glasgow and is littered with myriad found and altered objects, such as glow-in-the-dark prayer beads, political flyers relating to the right-wing Indian organisation RSS and the Glasgow Indian Workers Union, and toilet roll printed with cartoonish images of Mughals and funeral flowers. This messy heavens references Kaur's interest in the dualism of the 'political-mystic', a figure from her ancestry straddling both political and spiritual liberation. Sitting on the large carpet below, we as visitors are invited to gather together and observe, as we might in a home or place of worship.

Linsey Young

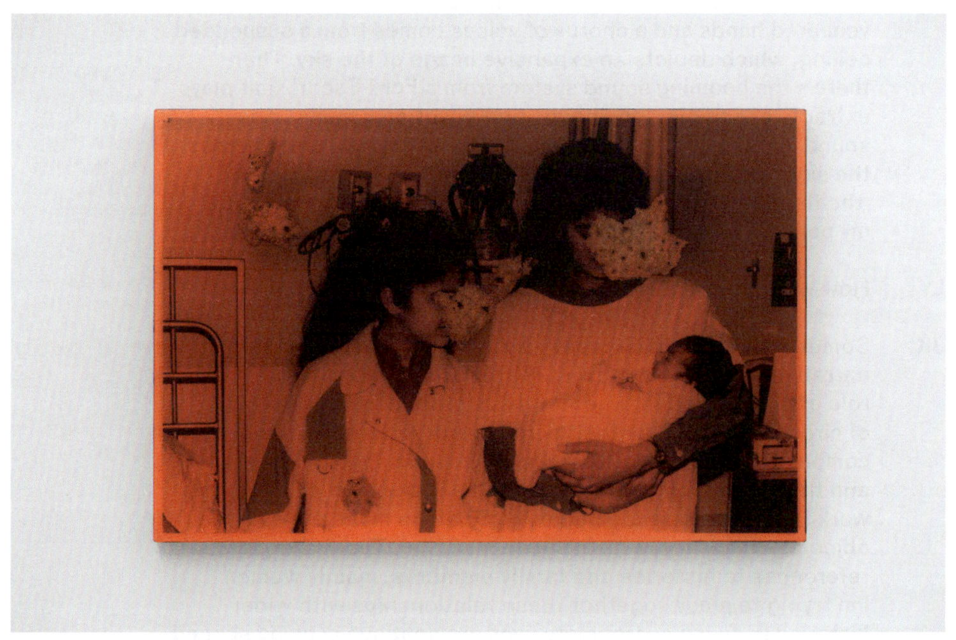

Untitled 2023, Resin, roti, photo on archive paper, 42 × 59.4 × 5 cm. © Jasleen Kaur.
Courtesy the artist and Hollybush Gardens, London, Photo: Eva Herzog

In Conversation

Linsey Young

You have been nominated for your exhibition *Alter Altar* at Tramway in Glasgow, and there are, of course, lots of striking images that audiences might have seen, but a central more intangible element is sound. Could you tell me about sound in relation to this body of work and your practice more broadly?

Jasleen Kaur

When I was invited to occupy the space at Tramway, I was thinking about how sound might hold the space, maybe because my reference point for huge spaces is the worship hall. I found myself mapping my relationship to the local area of Pollokshields, because it was once my neighbourhood and I wanted to speak alongside it, specifically to the building next door, which is a worship space that I have a really intimate relationship to. I wanted to think about what we are devoted to.

When you walk into the gallery, sound is emitted from various sculptures. There's the repetitive hum of a harmonium that sits in relation to an image of land being given back from one religious community to another for a mosque to be built. There's the chiming of worship bells from gesturing veneered hands and a chorus of voices comes from a suspended ceiling, which depicts an expansive image of the sky. Then there's the booming sound system from a Ford Escort that plays extracts of sampled pop songs and devotional music. The sound, along with all the other objects that are littered across the sky, and images of community solidarity positioned on the floor are like citations. They're reference points to how my political education was formed or unformed, growing up.

LY   How was your political education formed or unformed?

JK   Sometimes it was in discreet ways. I think a lot about the narratives you inherit, how they are maintained and the role of images in this, whether mass produced or taken out of circulation, because they were considered a threat. The composer Pauline Oliveros talks about 'listening behind you' and this has become a process for me in the studio. In this work I play with how ideologies circulate in mundane everyday objects: a necklace, a newspaper, a sticker. There are references to histories and family members, mainly women. I'm trying to piece together these relationships with wider histories because our intimate lives are continually being shaped and marred by these bigger forces.

    JK

I've been really fixated on a particular period of my ancestry, where devotional singing was done in more plural ways across what we now understand as religious categories. I'm interested in how and why this has been dismantled. For me, this music practice I've inherited is one way I understand the ramifications of colonialism, borders, nation building exercises or political and religious reform. There's something fugitive about song that I'm drawn to — you can burn a library full of books but you can't burna sound which is passed down through oral tradition.

LY   Are you talking about people who would use singing or sound as part of worship, which was then stopped by other forces, so it was a form of resistance to continue the practice?

JK   I'd like to think of it as a form of resistance, yes. My relationship to singing is not just a spiritual one, it's a political one. Ariella Azoulay talks about 'potential history' and when I started to read her book of the same title it gave me language for something I find myself doing, salvaging anti-imperial histories to think about how to live now and in the future.

The sound of the chorus from under the sky was produced with voice practitioner Marged Siôn. It was transformative because my relationship to singing has always been mediated through the family or religious community. Marged comes to singing through the Welsh (Cymraeg) language chapel so we both have a relationship to voice through worship and the liberating possibilities of singing together. Over months we worked through a series of somatic exercises to create space in the body to resource sound from. There was a doubling up of imagining spaces to resource us — the ones in our bodies and the one I was creating in the gallery. What you hear is Marged guiding me through the exercises in a recording studio but set to traditional raag scales. The vocal exercises are all facilitated through the movement of the body. It's not a performance, but a practice.

LY   It always feels to me that there's a strong collaborative element to your work. I'm thinking specifically of the publication project *Be Like Teflon* or the performances of *Gut Feelings Meri Jaan*, but also about the way an audience's body interacts with the work, sitting on a carpet enveloped in sound. Could you tell me a little bit about the role of collaboration within the work?

JK   I think a lot about holding people. How can I make a place that someone wants to spend time in? The carpet is a bid for intimacy, I'm longing for people to congregate.

Sometimes through my work I am facilitating a group to generate knowledge to produce a toolkit for a specific community or I'm gathering voices as a counter narrative.

Sometimes this is made visible and sometimes not. During the run of the show at Tramway, the gallery was used as a space for groups to convene — for prayer, voice workshops, reading groups, and family activities, often facilitated by local grassroots organisations. I was on maternity leave at the time and so it felt like an opportunity to build on the relationships Tramway already had with the local community, to hand over resources to those groups and turn the gallery into a functioning space.

LY   Having initially studied metalwork and jewellery, presumably with the production of small objects, you now work across a huge range of materials, including textiles, wood and cars, that are often substantial in scale. Could you talk about your relationship to material?

JK   It's nice to be asked this question, because I sometimes overlook it, maybe because I studied in the crafts where material and process was such a huge focus. I've always been attracted to material subterfuge — the faux, the veneer, the facade — and the places you find these materials are the kinds of places I grew up in. My formal education was this deep schooling in jewellery and metal; we'd collect metal dust and transform it back into a billet and then turn it into wire, and at some point, this kind of precision wasn't important to me anymore.

        I developed a cut and paste approach to making, that in hindsight allowed me to pull in historical references or material references more immediately, more effectively. Like three dimensional collage. Quite early in my practice I also realised I could play with legibility. Tina Campt talks about *'resist[ing] the lures and seductions of an easy reading'* and I think in this body of work there's a generosity but there's also a refusal. Information is coded in objects or concealed deliberately as a tactic, legible to some but not to everyone.

To access Jasleen's Turner Prize reading and play-list, please visit: https://www.tate.org.uk/ whats-on/tate-britain/turner-prize-2024

                                JK

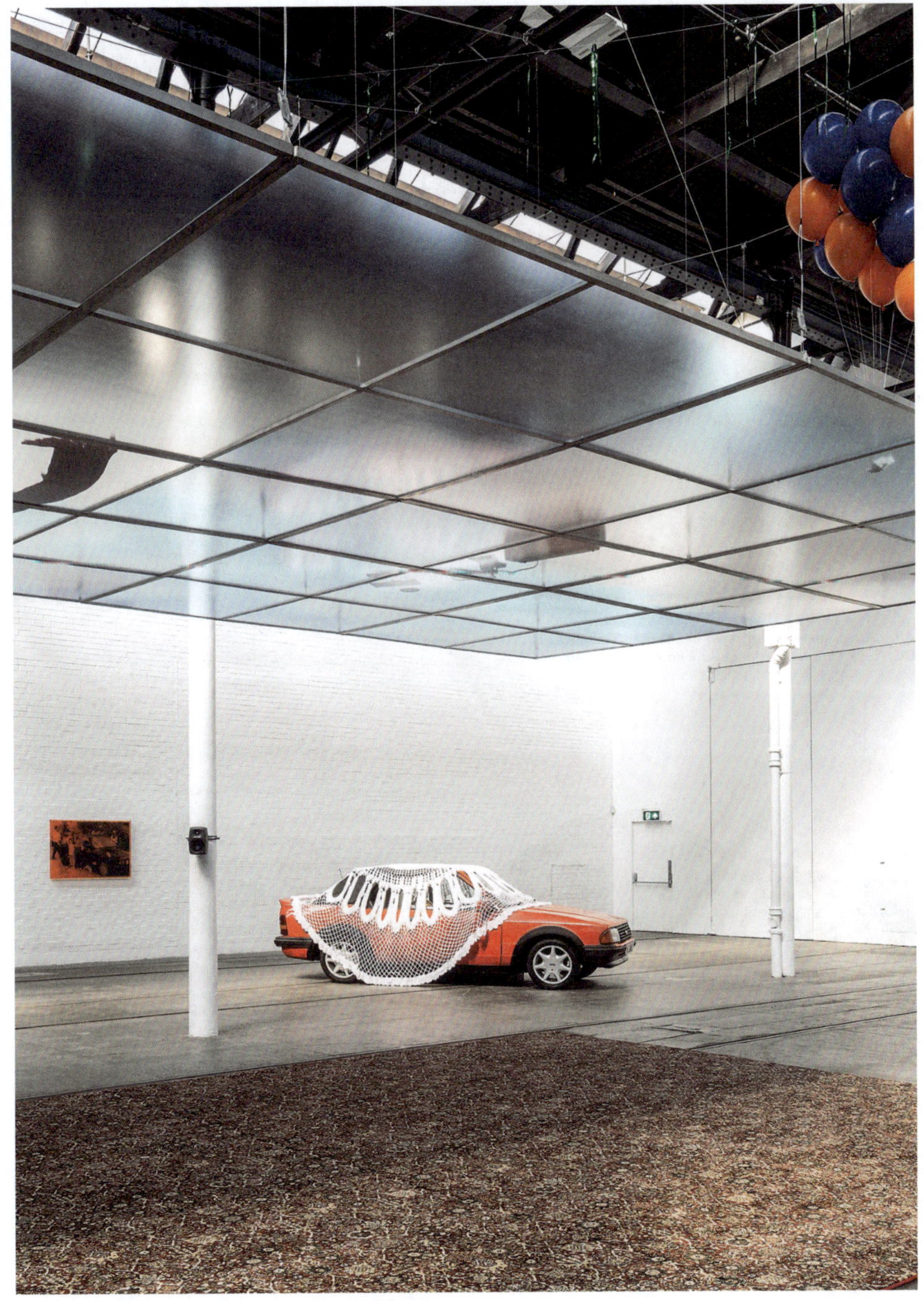

Alter Altar, installation view, Tramway, Glasgow, 2023.
Courtesy Tramway, Glasgow. Photo: Keith Hunter

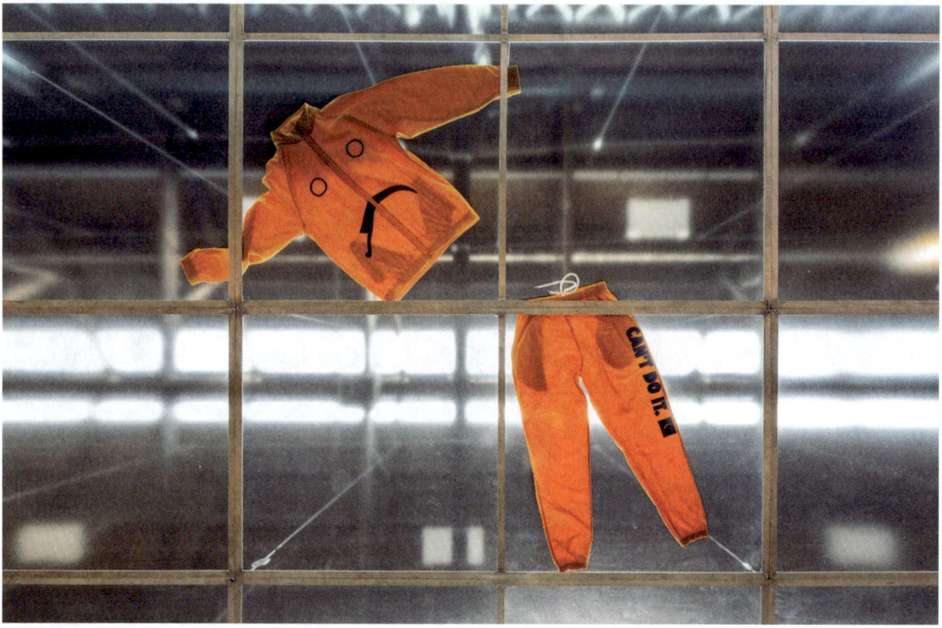

Alter Altar, installation view, Tramway, Glasgow, 2023.
Courtesy Tramway, Glasgow. Photo: Keith Hunter

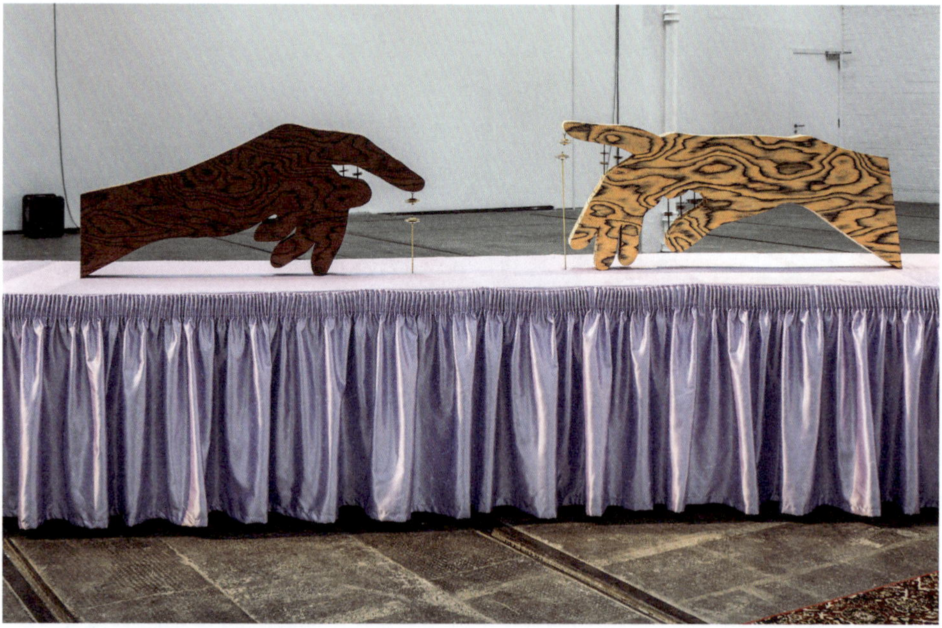

Alter Altar, installation view, Tramway, Glasgow, 2023.
Courtesy Tramway, Glasgow. Photo: Keith Hunter

JK

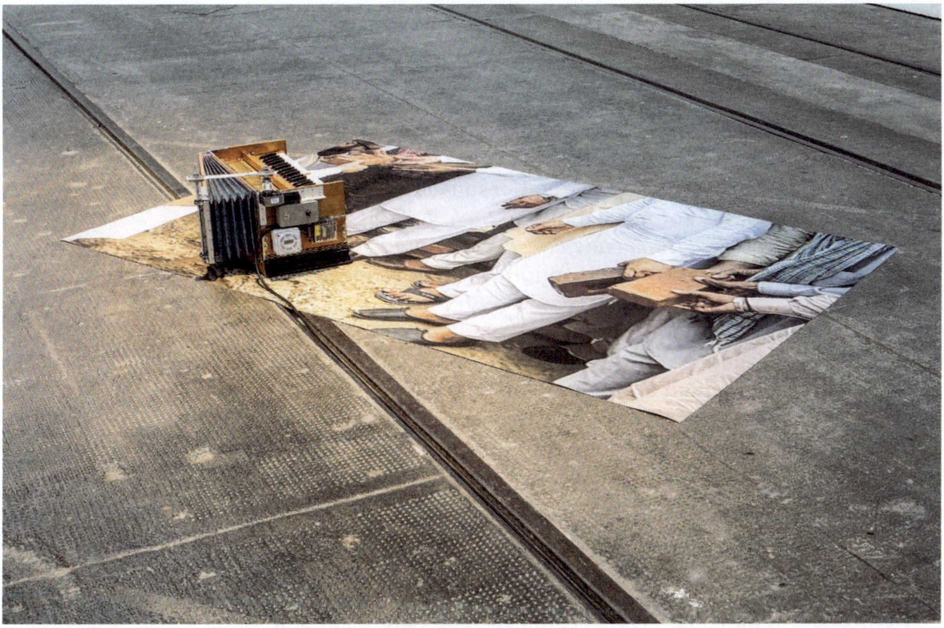

Alter Altar, installation view, Tramway, Glasgow, 2023.
Courtesy Tramway, Glasgow. Photo: Keith Hunter

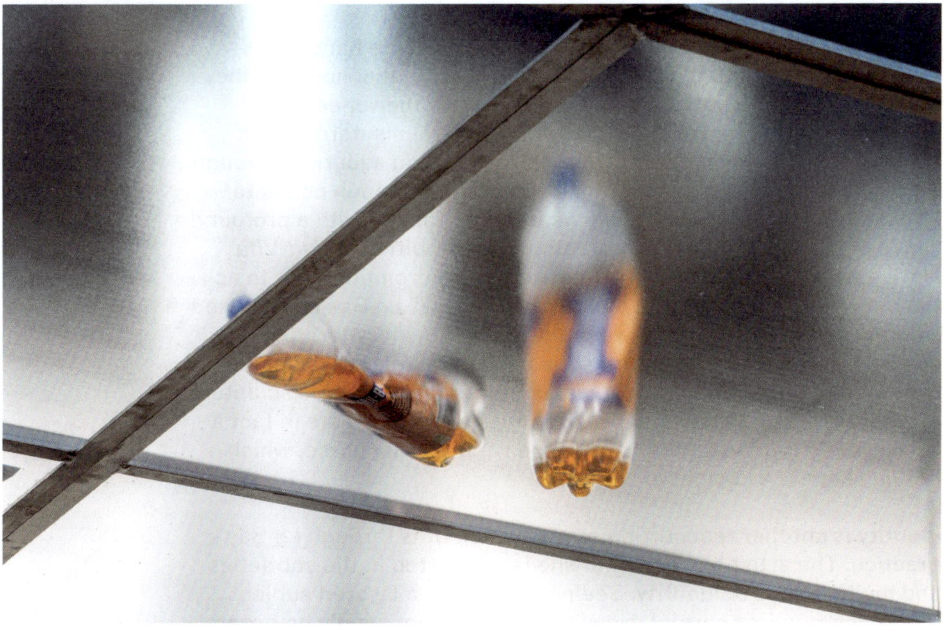

Alter Altar, installation view, Tramway, Glasgow, 2023.
Courtesy Tramway, Glasgow. Photo: Keith Hunter

Delaine Le Bas

Delaine Le Bas is an artist whose work delves into the complexities of identity, belonging, and cultural heritage. Through her powerful visual language, she addresses themes of marginalisation, resilience, and the interplay between personal and collective narratives. Nominated for her exhibition *Incipit Vita Nova. Here Begins The New Life/A New Life Is Beginning* at Secession, the artist takes us on a journey through loss and renewal.

Le Bas's work uses various mediums, including painting, drawing, film and performance, to create immersive installations which address nationhood, land and belonging. Her work focuses on political and social concerns as well as private and emotional aspects of her life, including her Roma heritage and the cultural history of her people. The artist's desire to challenge stereotypes and provoke thought is platformed by her use of textiles, found objects, and vibrant colours, to create environments that invite viewers to question their preconceptions and engage with stories which may be unfamiliar. Le Bas, who studied fashion and textiles at Central Saint Martins, incorporates various textiles and clothing within her works, which are often embroidered, hand painted, collaged and embellished and also act as costumes during the performative part of her practice.

The vibrancy of these textiles and delicate, intricate handling of fabrics, draws viewers in with their 'pretty' aesthetic, however they reveal on closer inspection what lurks beneath the veneer of Le Bas's practice — a preoccupation with loss, dreams, terrors and trauma. Le Bas's immense installation takes us on a journey through a psychic landscape, from nightmare to dream, through chaos to ultimately a transformation. The installation is laced with a profound sense of loss and grief. When creating the exhibition *Incipit Vita Nova*, Le Bas's nan had recently passed away, prompting her to ask the question, '"How can you make art in chaos?" Le Bas has created a shrine and memorial to the recently departed, incorporating symbols, relics and remade precious mementos relating to lost loved ones. A pair of red baby shoes, placed underneath a fabric sculpture of a horse (representative of her grandfather's horse,) are in fact a replica of Le Bas's own first baby shoes and a china horse, which her nan kept in a cabinet in her home.

Identity is another reoccurring strand which runs through Le Bas's practice. The artist has said that she is interested in the subtleties and multiplicities of identity. Seeing identity as a layered subject, one which requires careful excavation and cannot simply be boxed or bracketed into stereotypes. Le Bas says, 'for me the term identity and what it means, and the boxes people are put in and who puts

DLB

who in the boxes and who actually labels the boxes as well' is incredibly important in understanding someone's identity and how they are perceived by others. Le Bas's work is layered in its meaning and in its physical materiality. Her installations are a testament to the beauty that can be found in diversity, urging a re-examination of the histories and identities that shape our world.

Le Bas has exhibited internationally, participating in significant exhibitions such as the Venice Biennale and the Prague Biennale. Her work is not only a reflection of her personal journey but also a voice for the broader experience of being on the 'outside'. Through her art, Le Bas invites us to explore many questions, including the fluid nature of identity and invites visitors to explore their own understanding of what this word means. These powerful stories challenge us to look beyond the surface and embrace the multiple strands of human experience.

Amy Emmerson Martin

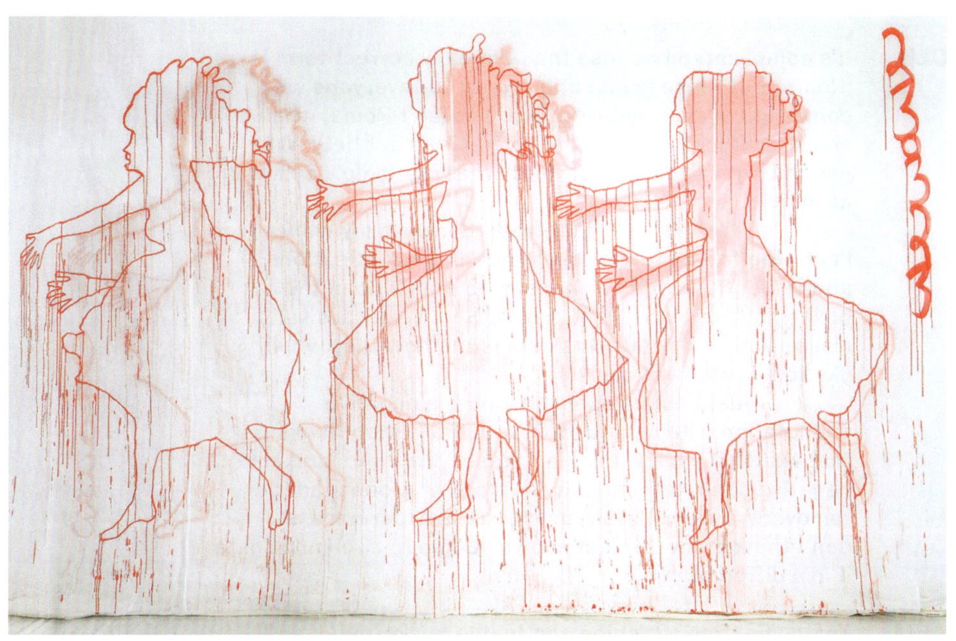

Photo © Iris Ranzinger

In Conversation

Amy Emmerson Martin

> You've spoken in the past about certain fixed stereotypes and how you like to push and play with them. How do you address your own identity? Do you get fed up with having to explain it all the time?

Delaine Le Bas

> It's generally that I have to start at point zero, and that's because people just don't know. So much of what is out there has been written from the outside looking in. That's the real problem. People won't like me saying this, but people think they have the right to tell me who I am.
>
> I'm only speaking on behalf of myself, not on behalf of a whole community that is often bundled together, and that is many different people. I'm just trying to tell my own story in my own way, from where I am. And that, for many people, isn't what they want to see.

AEM Thinking about language, what are your thoughts and feelings about words used to address your identity, what they mean to you, and how they relate to your life and wider practice?

DLB It's complicated because the politically correct term is 'Roma', but Roma is just one group. For everyone who comes under that umbrella, but who isn't Roma, what about their identity? It's this question of subtlety: Who has the right to call who what? What rights do we have as individuals?

> That's what I'm interested in with my work. I'm trying to pull these things out and ask questions about identity, what it means, who puts who in the boxes and who labels the boxes. So, I've always said, maybe you just need to ask someone how they would like to be referred to.
>
> Just because someone puts a negative connotation with a word, do you actually stop thinking that word? Does the thinking around the word, and any negative connotations that the word has, does that get removed? Unfortunately, my personal experience is, I don't think it does, it just allows people to circumnavigate it in a different way.

AEM You come from a fashion and textile background, and often use fabrics, including clothing in your artworks. What do you like about working with textiles?

DLB   Well, textile has a flexibility. You can expand and contract it,
           you can make something that is site-specific, but then you can
           change the construction in a different environment. My work
           Witch Hunt 2009, for example, has travelled all over the place.
               For me, choosing to work with textiles was about
           a number of things. I could work on it wherever I was, and
           it packs away quite small. The other thing was, very often, I
           was being asked to do shows where budgets were minimal.
           If I could take a big installation in just two suitcases, that
           eradicated transport costs.
               I used to use a lot of reclaimed materials in my work,
           and I was always interested in what was actually on those
           reclaimed materials. So, it's much more about what was
           already embedded in the textile in terms of the print or the
           pattern, and what that actually meant, and the colours of
           things as well.

AEM   When I look at your work, it can feel like collage – the cutting
           and stitching of different textiles. What's the thought
           process behind it? Is it simply, I like that material or that pattern,
           or docs seeing these two things together create a tension?

DLB   Now I make everything from scratch, but when I was using
           found materials, a fabric would trigger something – it can
           just be about colour, or it might be a patch that had some
           wording on it.
               I'm also interested in the loaded imagery that we
           are surrounded by from a young age, and what impact that
           has, how it feeds into our subconscious. The found things
           were about, 'what if you put that with that', what if you
           juxtapose an Action Man quilt and 1950s nursery curtains
           with depictions of gruesome fairy tales and you make those
           as a hanging that goes behind a sort of Madonna figure ...
           So what is the reading of it going to be? But also what's
           the other narrative, what's it trying to say about power
           structures, about pure brute force and religious power as well?
               Looking at materials in those ways was also about
           reclaiming and recycling, and using mainly clothes and things
           that were my own. They're still in a lot of the works now
           – bits of clothing that are mine that are no longer possible
           to wear because I've worn them so much. So, they end up
           being in parts of the work.

AEM   It's not just textiles that you work with, it's film, text and
           audio too. You've said before that you believe everyone
           is entitled to a cultural life, and I feel that there is a desire
           in your practice to make works inclusive for everyone.
           Do you think working with a variety of different media helps
           with that?

DLB   It's actually in the Declaration of Human Rights that everyone
        is entitled to a cultural life. I think more people should know
        what's on it – it's a very important document.
                For me, when I was growing up, I was introduced to
        films through my grandmother and my great-uncle, and music
        was very important. So, it wasn't really visual arts that were
        the things that were attracting me to a cultural life. But there
        were doorways for me into it.
                I'm interested in creating different doorways,
        because I know that for some people, they really respond to
        sound, for example. But for others sound might be difficult.
        Fabric is another way of engaging with people because it's
        not behind glass. So, you are physically in the same space
        as it. For me it's about creating different entry points. That's
        how I found my way, eventually, into art.

AEM   Collaboration is often part of your practice, and for many
        years you collaborated with your husband. What does
        collaboration give to your work, and why is it important to
        have those collaborations running through each of your
        projects and exhibitions?

DLB   There are a lot of things I can do, but there are a lot of
        things I can't do. I can take film footage, but I can't edit
        the film. I can know that I want a sound, but I can't make it.
        So, for instance, Justin Langlands, who I have worked with
        for a long time now, does all the soundscapes. And I work
        with Lincoln Cato on the sonography, and he designs the
        sculptural furniture for each exhibition. Hera S Santos does
        the performance with me. Then there's László Farkas, who
        I work with on films, and I used to work with my son on films too.
        I still use the same camera that I've had for years. It's got this
        strange fault on it, but it's almost become my trademark.
                It's about having conversations with people, and
        talking about the seeds of the work, and then enabling
        something to develop between us.
                These relationships are also really important to
        me, and I feel that is embedded in the work. I know the word
        'care' gets bandied around a lot now, but I feel that there is
        a lot of love and care between us and hopefully, you can feel
        that in the work.

AEM   Could you talk about the performance part of your practice
        and how it relates to your installations?

DLB   I can't really separate it out from the work – all of it is one big
        thing. When we did the show at Secession in Vienna, which
        will form the work shown at the Turner Prize, we opened it with
        a performance, and the space was only opened once the

performance had taken place. So, very often it acts as the starting point for the show actually being open. I don't see any separation between any of the things really, the sounds, the film, the costumes, the work, the installation, it's all one big thing.

AEM   I wanted to ask about your sketchbooks. You are always drawing, carrying a book around with you. Do you carry more than one?

DLB   Yes, usually I've got my diary, and two other books. I write as well – it might just be a bit of a conversation or I might just see something that I want to note down. For me, it's very important because working from my house and not having a studio, the books have become like an archive I can delve back into when I finally got the chance to make the work. So yes, they are constantly ongoing.

AEM   What are you currently enjoying outside of visual art? What music are you listening to?

DLB   Music is a difficult one for me because I listen to different things all the time. Radio 3 is great because they don't have so much news on. Not that I don't want to know what's going on in the world, but I struggle with the news sometimes.

I bought a Sun Ra album a little while ago, and I've got an old Malcolm McLaren album out at the moment. I inherited my late husband's record collection which contains a lot of Northern Soul. So, it's really varied. Historically, Poly Styrene from X-Ray Spex has been massive, so that has to come into it somewhere... sorry everyone!

AEM   What do you hope that visitors who come to the Turner Prize will feel or think from having seen your work?

DLB   Well, the piece that is going to be at Tate for the Turner Prize is *Incipit Vita Nova*, which translates to 'a new life begins' or 'a new life is beginning'. My grandmother was dying when I was thinking about making the work, and I was spending a lot of time up at night, when the shadows and the sounds and everything is very different. I was thinking about how to make art during a time of chaos.

I went through a very dark period of my life, and for many people at this moment in time, and on different parts of this planet, they are not in a good place. You can be in a dark place but you can get through it. It's quite beautiful.

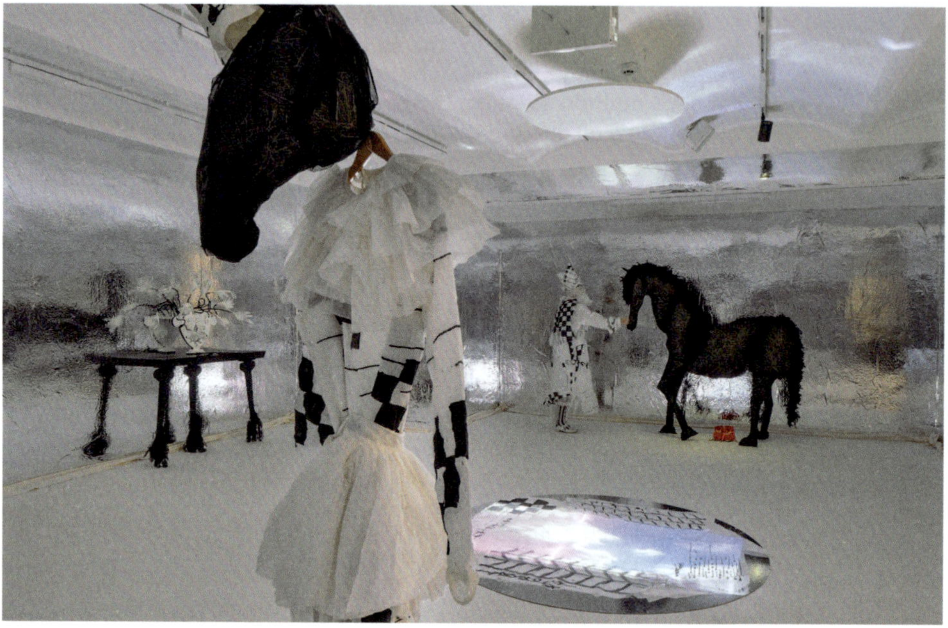

Installation view of Delaine Le Bas, Incipit Vita Nova. Here Begins The New Life/A New Life Is Beginning at Secession, Vienna 2023. Courtesy of Secession, Vienna. Photo © Iris Ranzinger

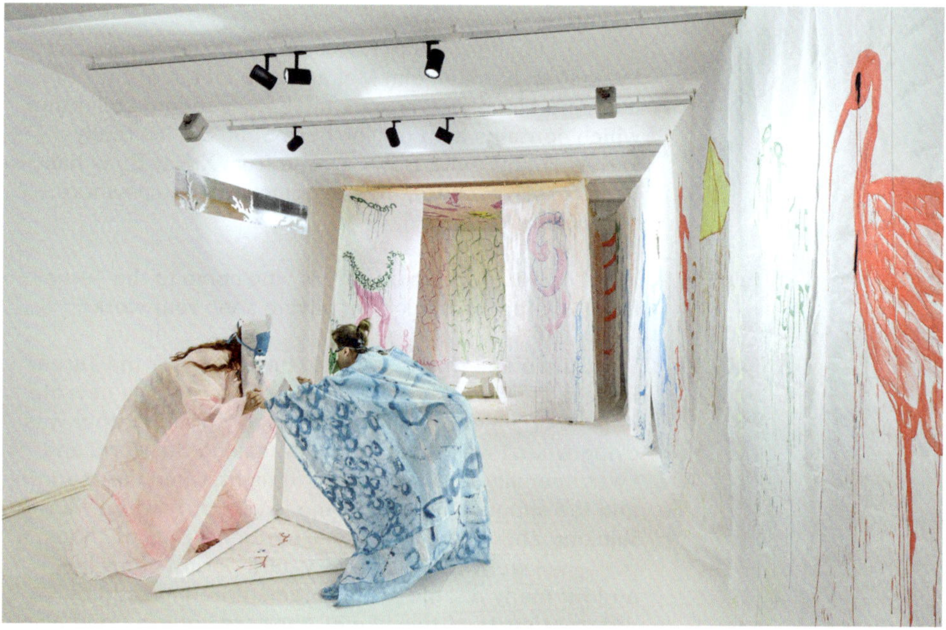

Installation view of Delaine Le Bas, Incipit Vita Nova. Here Begins The New Life/A New Life Is Beginning at Secession, Vienna 2023. Courtesy of Secession, Vienna. Photo © Iris Ranzinger

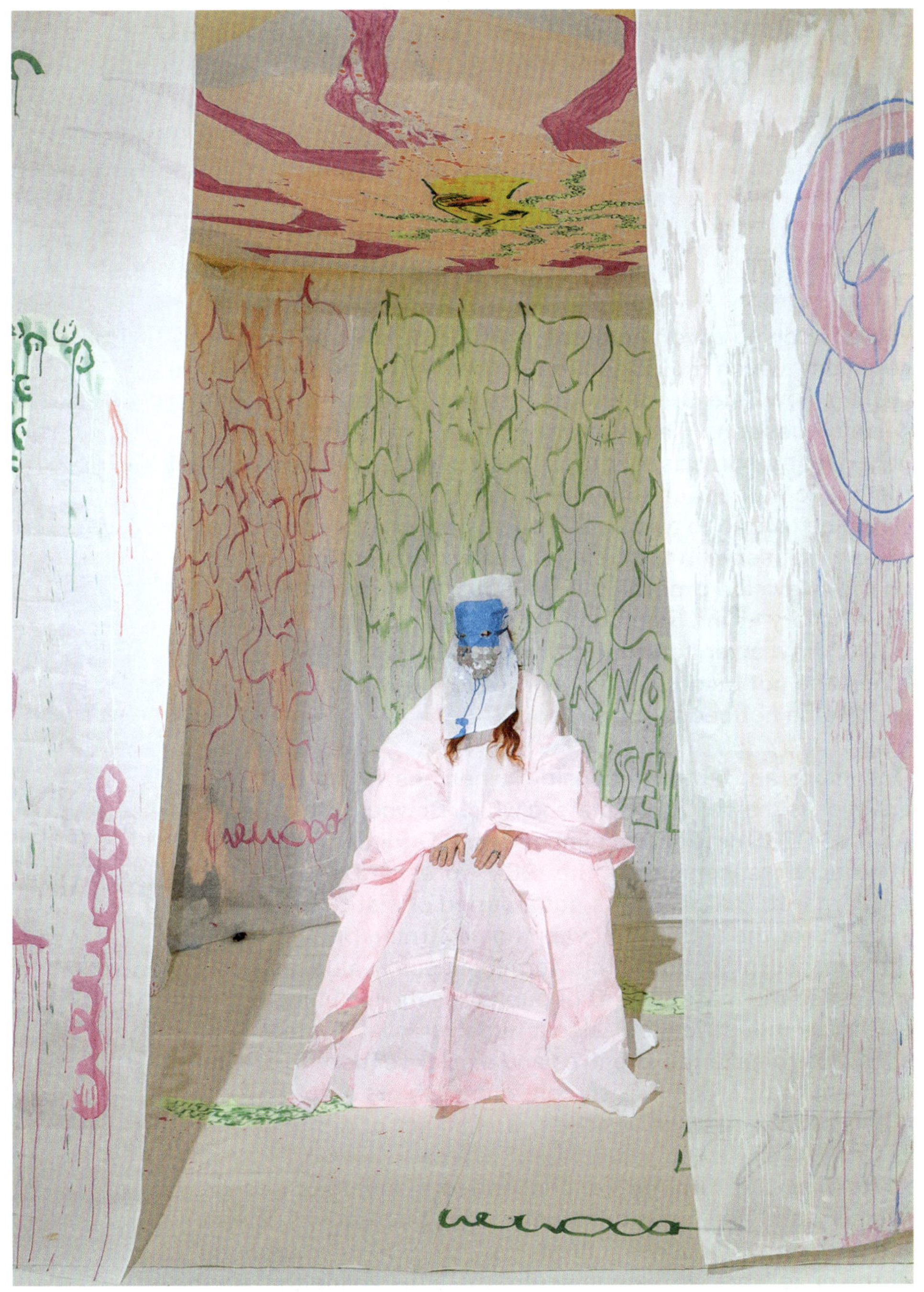

Installation view of Delaine Le Bas, Incipit Vita Nova. Here Begins The New Life/A New Life Is Beginning at Secession, Vienna 2023. Courtesy of Secession, Vienna. Photo © Iris Ranzinger

Stop, Look, Listen: The Turner Prize at 40
Nathalie Olah

While watching coverage of the first Turner Prize award ceremony, which took place in 1984 at what was then the Tate Gallery, now Tate Britain, I was struck by the persistence of certain questions. Those in attendance – mainly curators, gallerists and broadsheet columnists – were concerned about the public perception of art: whether the shortlisted works would be legible to a wide audience, and what function the prize might serve in the field of creative expression. Speaking on the television programme *Omnibus*, the director of the Tate Gallery at the time, Alan Bowness, said that the prize would 'draw attention to the work of artists, which would otherwise not be noticed.' But why did the work of artists need to be noticed by more people?

One important factor to consider when answering that question is the political climate in which Bowness was speaking. As the 2023 Turner Prize winner Jesse Darling pointed out in his acceptance speech, the 1980s, presided over in Britain by Margaret Thatcher, was not a period of institutional support for the arts. Profit was the governing principle of the age, usurping most other forms of social value, as we witnessed the mass sell-off of public assets, including housing and many industries, but also a huge removal of state subsidies to galleries, theatres and similar venues. To create an event that forced British contemporary art onto the mainstream news agenda then, was an act of defiance.

At its best, the Turner Prize challenged a climate of intense cynicism and it allowed different modes of creativity to enter the public consciousness. From 1987 to 1994, all recipients of the prize were working in sculpture, a discipline that, in the twentieth century at least, was informed by manual industry and public art. One stand-out example is *Untitled (House)* by Rachel Whiteread, which won the prize in 1993. Whiteread's concrete cast of a three-storey house was exhibited *in situ* in Tower Hamlets, East London, and combined formal innovation and rhetorical genius to create a perfect metaphor and visual pun for the way in which property ownership had in many ways calcified the home, transforming places of life and memory into assets and faceless objects.

Whiteread was often associated with the Young British Artists (YBAs), a group that emerged in the late 1980s and was defined by the members' humble backgrounds, incendiary attitudes, and quite paradoxically, popularity among multi-millionaire collectors. Another notable YBA-affiliated artist is Gillian Wearing, whose video work *60 Minutes Silence* won in 1997 and offered a subtle commentary on class and power by showing a group portrait of actors dressed as police officers wince and fidget under the artist's gaze. Initially, the YBAs, who dominated the Turner Prize throughout the 1990s, would seem to indicate a period of class consciousness and another joyful challenge to the elitism of the establishment — but this impression was somewhat tarnished by the wealth and status they often gained.

Film and video installation work started to appear on the prize shortlists more and more in the late 1990s and early 2000s. It was relatively easy to access and produce, and, in sharing a visual language with more popular modes of entertainment and advertising of the time, also able to comment effectively on the audio-visual aspects of modern life. Douglas Gordon, who won in 1996, distorts perception and alters the relationship between film and viewer. His film *24 Hour Psycho* transforms a cinematic classic, reducing it to a series of stills that spans a 24-hour period, and forcing a re-evaluation of the broadcast technology — its tropes and manipulation tactics — that we had readily invited into our homes. In the prize-winning *Deadpan*, Steve McQueen reimagines the iconic hurricane scene from Buster Keaton's 1928 film *Steamboat Bill Jr.*, in which he narrowly escapes the falling façade of a house. Where Keaton clambers about and runs away in shock, McQueen is stuck — repeating the scene in laceless shoes that prevent him from running. It is a comment on the invisibility of Black people in the

American cinematic tradition, but also of choice, panic and
anxiety.

In what serves as a very good example of the interdependency
between art and civic life, Chris Ofili won the prize in 1998
with a body of work that included the painting *No Woman No
Cry*, a representation of Doreen Lawrence, whose teenage
son, Stephen, was murdered in a racist attack in 1993. In
the work, Doreen is depicted in tears, while the words *RIP
Stephen Lawrence* are painted in phosphorescent paint, in
what many interpret to be a reference to the police cover up
over the murder investigation. Ofili's portrait was acquired
by Tate in 1999 and is now held in the national collection,
reminding subsequent generations of the white supremacy
still prevalent in Britain, as well as the institutional racism
of the Metropolitan police as identified in the Macpherson
Report.

From this partial selection of previous winners, it would be
tempting to assume that the prize rewards social justice
movements, or that contemporary art needs to be justified
along the lines of social transformation, but this is not
the case. Given the confusion, the prize could do more, perhaps,
to explain that the discipline of art is always concerned
with formal constraints and is a dialogue between the traditional
and the contemporary — that every work is either an act of
conformity or resistance to whatever its chosen artform has
been used to celebrate and uphold in the past.

With the turn of the century and the publication in English of
the influential text *Relational Art* by the French critic Nicholas
Bourriaud, came an emphasis on space, performance and
the role and complicity of the audience. In 2001, Jeremy
Deller won the prize for *The Battle of Orgreave (An Injury to
One is an Injury to All)*, a re-enactment of one of the most
violent and pivotal moments in the 1980s miners' strikes.
In 2005, Simon Starling was awarded the accolade for his
Shedboatshed, in which he discovered a shed-like structure
on the banks of the Rhine, dismantled it and used part to
construct a boat on which to transport the rest, reassembling
the structure eventually at a gallery in Switzerland. While
in 2010, Susan Philipsz won for her work *Lowlands*, a
sixteenth-century Scottish lament that was played under

three bridges over Glasgow's River Clyde before being adapted to be shown at Tate Britain. Although it is difficult to draw a direct line between these winning entries, all gave pause about the bounds and limits of art, the integrity of the art object and the relationship between artist and public. It is fair to say that in more recent years, forms have started to proliferate and merge. No one discipline seems to dominate, but artists working across a multiplicity of platforms and technologies, including sculpture, video, performance, and painting, and many of them working in groups and collectives too, are recognised more for their ingenuity in response to the issues of today. The architecture organisation Assemble was awarded the prize in 2016 for a regeneration project in the impoverished area of Granby, Liverpool, a work speaking to the ongoing effects of economic austerity, while the 2021 list of nominees was made up exclusively of collectives, in what felt like a challenge to our individualistic culture and to the myth of the artist as a lone genius. These included Black Obsidian Sound System, Cooking Sections, and the winner, Array Collective, who produced a body of work in protest to social issues including abortion and gay rights in Northern Ireland.

If we return to the words of Alan Bowness, how much is the prize today drawing attention to the artists it celebrates, and how much is it acting as a barometer of broader currents within British art, and society? This year there's a question of resourcefulness. Jasleen Kaur mines an archive of the dispossessed in her work, composed as it is of scraps and salvaged materials. Romani artist Delaine Le Bas weaves tapestries from found objects. Claudette Johnson's intimate depictions of Black women and men demonstrate the struggle for recognition in a society that is built on a system of Black oppression. Pio Abad tries to make sense of histories distorted through the gaze of Western colonialism. Publicity, if it is still a motivator for the prize, is only sought for the purposes of giving people an opportunity to reflect on their present reality. An art prize might not be able to make any material change to the world around it, but it can and does serve as a guide and indicator of where we all, collectively, might be headed.

Turner Prize Winners and Nominees

* Winner

1984
Malcolm Morley*
Richard Deacon
Gilbert and George
Howard Hodgkin
Richard Long

1985
Howard Hodgkin*
Terry Atkinson
Tony Cragg
Ian Hamilton Finlay
Milena Kalinovska
John Walker

1986
Gilbert and George*
Art & Language
Victor Burgin
Derek Jarman
Stephen McKenna
Bill Woodrow

1987
Richard Deacon*
Patrick Caulfield
Helen Chadwick
Richard Long
Declan McGonagle
Thérèse Oulton

1988
Tony Cragg*
Lucian Freud
Richard Hamilton
Richard Long
David Mach
Boyd Webb
Alison Wilding
Richard Wilson

1989
Richard Long*
Gillian Ayres
Lucian Freud
Giuseppe Penone
Paula Rego
Sean Scully
Richard Wilson

1990
Prize suspended

1991
Anish Kapoor*
Ian Davenport
Fiona Rae
Rachel Whiteread

1992
Grenville Davey*
Damien Hirst
David Tremlett
Alison Wilding

1993
Rachel Whiteread*
Hannah Collins
Vong Phaophanit
Sean Scully

1994
Antony Gormley*
Willie Doherty
Peter Doig
Shirazeh Houshiary

1995
Damien Hirst*
Mona Hatoum
Callum Innes
Mark Wallinger

1996
Douglas Gordon*
Craigie Horsfield
Gary Hume
Simon Patterson

1997
Gillian Wearing*
Christine Borland
Angela Bulloch
Cornelia Parker

1998
Chris Ofili*
Tacita Dean
Cathy de Monchaux
Sam Taylor-Johnson

1999
Steve McQueen*
Tracey Emin
Steven Pippin
Jane and Louise Wilson

2000
Wolfgang Tillmans*
Glenn Brown
Michael Raedecker
Tomoko Takahashi

2001
Martin Creed*
Richard Billingham
Isaac Julien
Mike Nelson

2002
Keith Tyson*
Fiona Banner
Liam Gillick
Catherine Yass

2003
Grayson Perry*
Jake and Dinos Chapman
Willie Doherty
Anya Gallaccio

2004
Jeremy Deller*
Kutluğ Ataman
Langlands and Bell
Yinka Shonibare

2005
Simon Starling*
Darren Almond
Gillian Carnegie
Jim Lambie

2006
Tomma Abts*
Phil Collins
Mark Titchner
Rebecca Warren

2007
Mark Wallinger*
Nathan Coley
Zarina Bhimji
Mike Nelson

2008
Mark Leckey*
Runa Islam
Goshka Macuga
Cathy Wilkes

2009
Richard Wright*
Enrico David
Roger Hiorns
Lucy Skaer

2010
Susan Philipsz*
Dexter Dalwood
Angela de la Cruz
The Otolith Group
(Anjalika Sagar and
Kodwo Eshun)

2011
Martin Boyce*
Karla Black
Hilary Lloyd
George Shaw

2012
Elizabeth Price*
Monster Chetwynd
Luke Fowler
Paul Noble

2013
Laure Prouvost *
Lynette Yiadom-Boakye
David Shrigley
Tino Sehgal

2014
Duncan Campbell*
Ciara Phillips
James Richards
Tris Vonna-Michell

2015
Assemble*
Bonnie Camplin
Janice Kerbel
Nicole Wermers

2016
Helen Marten*
Michael Dean
Anthea Hamilton
Josephine Pryde

2017
Lubaina Himid*
Rosalind Nashashibi
Hurvin Anderson
Andrea Büttner

2018
Charlie Prodger*
Forensic Architecture
Naeem Mohaiemen
Luke Willis Thompson

2019
Lawrence Abu Hamdan*
Helen Cammock*
Tai Shani*
Oscar Murillo*

2020
Cancelled / Bursaries:
Oreet Ashery
Liz Johnson Artur
Shawanda Corbett
Jamie Crewe
Sean Edwards
Sidsel Meineche Hansen
Ima-Abasi Okon
Imran Perretta
Alberta Whittle
Arika

2021
Array Collective*
B.O.S.S
Cooking Sections
Gentle/Radical
Project Art Works

2022
Veronica Ryan*
Heather Phillipson
Ingrid Pollard
Sin Wai Kin

2023
Jesse Darling*
Ghislaine Leung
Rory Pilgrim
Barbara Walker

2024
*TBA
Pio Abad
Claudette Johnson
Jasleen Kaur
Delaine Le Bas